LEARNING TO READ MADE EASY
BOOK 1

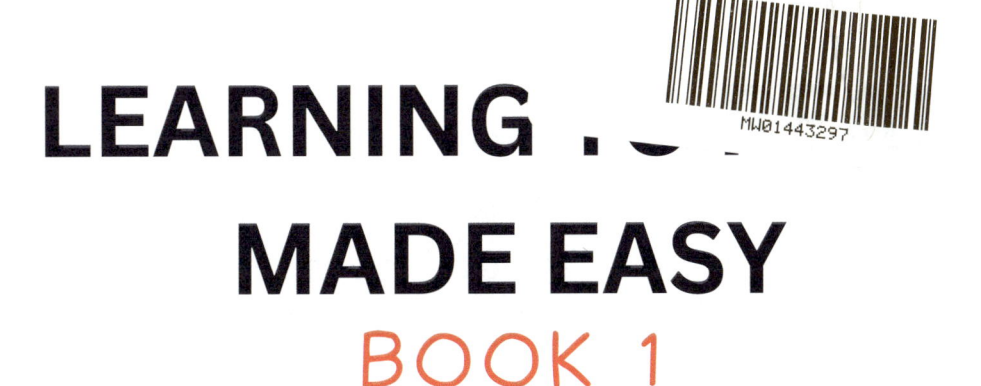

Text Copyright © 2024 Dale Children's Print

All rights reserved- Dale Children's Print . No part of this publication mat be reproduced, distributed, or transmitted in any form or by any means, including photocopying, recording, or other electronic or mechanical methods, without the prior written permission of the publisher, except in the case of brief quotations embodied in critical reviews and certain other non-commercial use permitted by copyright law.

IISBN-13 : 979-8338681077

For more information:

Email: daleschildrenprint@gmail.com

Youtube: LearningtoReadMadeEasy

A review here to share your experience would be greatly appreciated:

"Welcome to "***Learning to Read Made Easy Book 1***', a reading manual designed to guide you in teaching your child the essential skill of reading! Learning to read can be a fun and rewarding experience for your child, and with your support and guidance, they will be well on their way to becoming a confident reader.

This manual provides step-by-step instructions and simple lessons that will have your child reading in no time.

Our approach is structured and easy to follow, with each stage building on the previous one.

- Learning of letter sounds
- Blending and decoding skills
- Build phonemic awareness
- Sight words recognition
- Develop fluency and comprehension skills

By following our manual, you will be able to:

- Support your child's individual learning needs
- Make reading an enjoyable and engaging experience
- Help your child develop a lifelong love of reading

Let's get started on this exciting journey and watch your child become a confident and proficient reader!"

Machelle.R.Shaw

Instructour's Guide

This book contains 2 units. For reference vowels are the letters 'a, e, i, o, u'. All the other letters are consonant letters(.eg. c s k, p).

UNIT 1: Consist of 10 lessons of consonant-vowel-consonant words(CVC). Example : cat

UNIT 2 : Consist of 8 lessons of consonant-vowel-consonant-consonant words. Example : cast

Each lesson consists of 3 sections:

Section A: In this section child learns letter sounds and practice blending the sounds to decode words. Repetition is very important.

Section B: In this section the child is given 2 sight words to memorize. Repetition is important.

Section C: In this section your child begins reading using the words from sections A and B.

There are also regular review for you to track your child's progress and to ensure they are retaining what they have learn.

N.B. Durations are given as guide, however as every child is unique so this may vary. Go with the pace of your child.

Tips

- Makes lesson fun by maintaining a positive attitude.
- You can make word cards or other material to enhance learning.
- Offer rewards to motivate your child and to celebrate their achievements.
- Whenever your child makes a mistake allow them to try again rather than offering the correct answer as your first response.

Use this as guide in producing the correct letter sounds.

/s/ as in sat	/b/ as in bat	/e/ as in egg
/m/ as in mat	/p/ as in pig	/f/ as in fish
/c/ as in cat	/i/ as in igloo	/j/ as in jug
/a/ as in ant	/g/ as in goat	/w/ as in watch
/t/ as in tag	/l/ as in light	/o/ as in orange
/r/ as in ran	/h/ as in hill	/u/ as in up
/v/ as in van	/k/ as in kite	/x/ as in axe
/n/ as in nut	/d/ as in dig	

Contents

Pages

SECTION 1   CVC words and Sight Word

Lesson 1	....	2 - 4
Lesson 2	....	5 - 7
Lesson 3	....	10 - 12
Lesson 4	....	13 - 15
Lesson 5	....	19 - 21
Lesson 6	....	22 - 24
Lesson 7	....	27 - 29
Lesson 8	....	30 - 32
Lesson 9	....	36 - 37
Lesson 10	....	39 - 41

SECTION 2   CVCC Words and Sight Words

Lesson 11	....	48 - 50
Lesson 12	....	51 - 53
Lesson 13	....	54 - 56
Lesson 14	....	58 - 60
Lesson 15	....	62 - 65
Lesson 16	....	66 - 68
Lesson 17	....	70 - 73
Lesson 18	....	74 - 76

UNIT 1

CVC
Short Vowel

Lesson 1A - Decoding

Instructor's Guide

DURATION:
3-5 days

OBJECTIVES:
- Produce and memorize sound for letters :
  s , m , c , a , t
- Blend sounds to decode cvc words.

Day 1-2
Instruct child to make the sound of each letter as they run their fingers across letters to learn and memorize the sounds
eg. s a t
Repeat several times. Then randomly touch letter and instruct child to make the letter sound.
e.g. t   m   s

Day 3-5
Instruct child to make the sounds and blend at the end
e.g.   s   a   t
sat

s → a → t   sat

s → a → t   sat

s → a → t   sat

m → a → t   mat

m → a → t   mat

m → a → t   mat

c → a → t   cat

c → a → t   cat

c → a → t   cat

Lesson 1B- Sight Words

Instructor's Guide

DURATION:
2 days

OBJECTIVE:
- Memorize the words 'the' and 'on'.

Instruct child to touch and say the words left to right. Repeat several times. Touch words randomly and instruct child say the words.

Instruct child to colour all 'the' in a colour of their choice and all 'on' in another colour of their choice.

The	on	the
The	on	the
The	on	the

The
on
The
the
on
on
The
the
on

Lesson 1C - Reading

Instructors Guide

DURATION:
2-3 days

OBJECTIVES:
- Read phrases and sentences given.
- Read for meaning.

Instruct child to read the phrases and sentences. Repeat several times.

Instruct child to identify and circle the picture that matches the sentence read.

| The | cat |

| the | mat |

| sat | on |

The cat sat.

The cat sat on the mat.

4

Lesson 2A - Decoding

Instructor's Guide

DURATION:
3-5 days

OBJECTIVES:
- Produce and memorize sound for letters:
   r, v, m, n, a
- Blend sounds to decode cvc words.

Day 1-2
Instruct child to make the sound of each letter as they run their fingers across letters to learn and memorize the sounds
eg. r a n
Repeat several times. Then randomly touch letter and instruct child to make the letter sound.
e.g. v m a

Day 3-5
Instruct child to make the sounds and blend at the end
e.g. r a n
ran

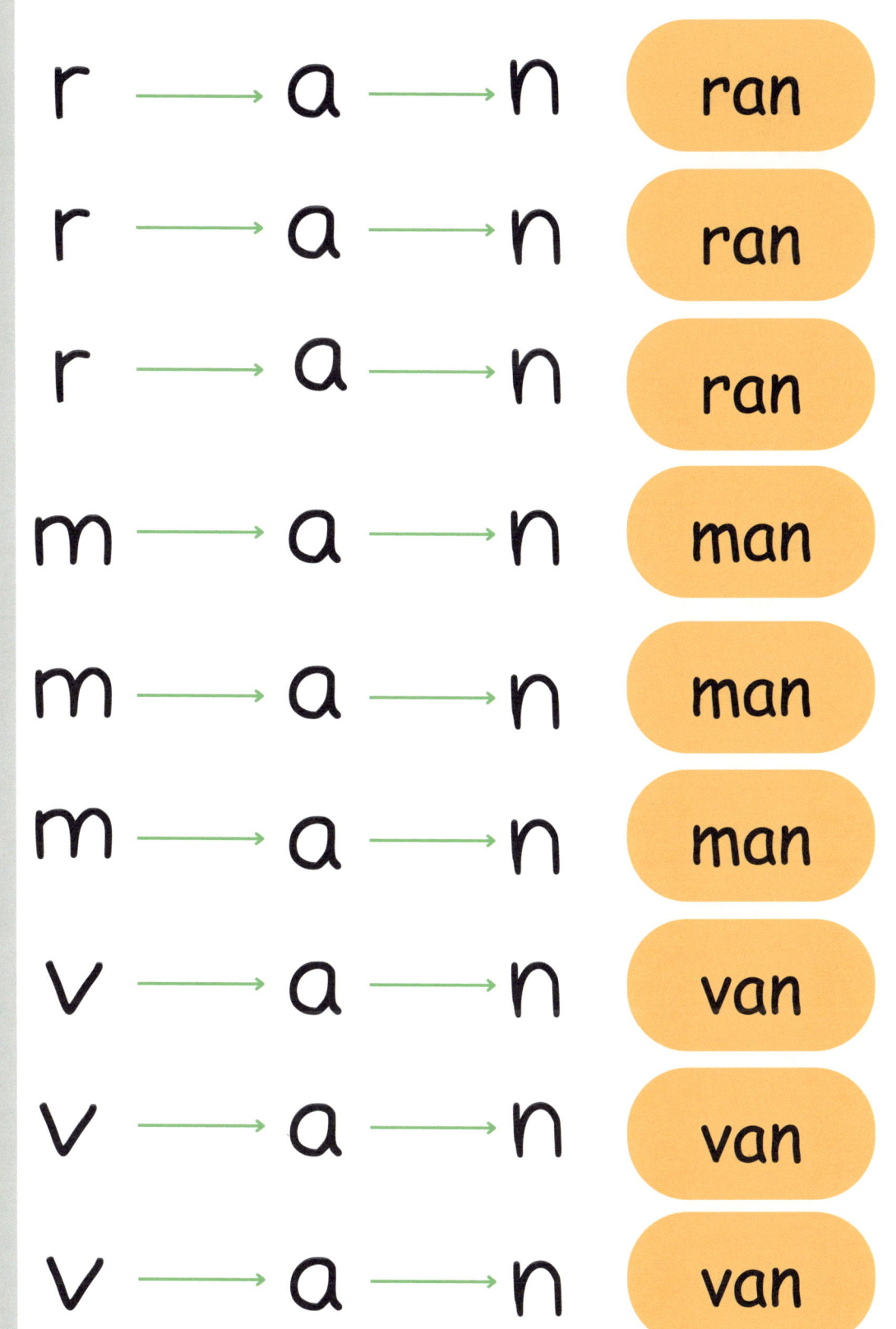

r → a → n ran
r → a → n ran
r → a → n ran
m → a → n man
m → a → n man
m → a → n man
v → a → n van
v → a → n van
v → a → n van

5

Lesson 2B - Sight Words

Instructor's Guide

DURATION:
2 days

OBJECTIVE:
- Memorize the words 'is' and 'in'.

Instruct child to touch and say the words left to right. Repeat several times. Touch words randomly and instruct child say the words.

Instruct child to colour all 'is' in a colour of their choice and all 'in' in another colour of their choice.

is	in	is
is	in	is
is	in	is

Clouds containing: is, in, is, in, is, in, is, is, in

Lesson 2C - Reading

Instructor's Guide

DURATION:
2-3 days

OBJECTIVES:
- Read phrases and sentences given.
- Read for meaning.

Instruct child to read the phrases and sentences. Repeat several times.

Instruct child to identify and circle the picture that matches the sentence read.

The	man		is	in

the	van

The man is in the van.

The man ran in the van.

7

Match the words to the picture

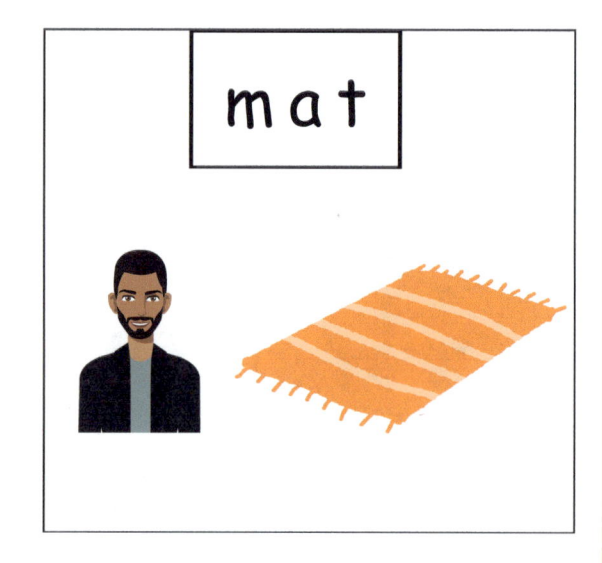

man	can
rat	mat
van	cat

Track Progress

The cat sat.

The cat sat on a mat.

The cat is on the mat.

The cat ran to the van.

The man is in the van.

1. What is on the mat?
2. Why do you think the cat run to the van?

Evaluation Table	1	2	3
Decoding Skill			
Sight Word Recognition			
Comprehension			
Comment :			

Lesson 3C - Reading

Instructor's Guide

DURATION:
2-3 days

OBJECTIVES:
- Read phrases and sentences given.
- Read for meaning.

Instruct child to read the phrases and sentences. Repeat several times.

Instruct child to identify and circle the picture that matches the sentence read.

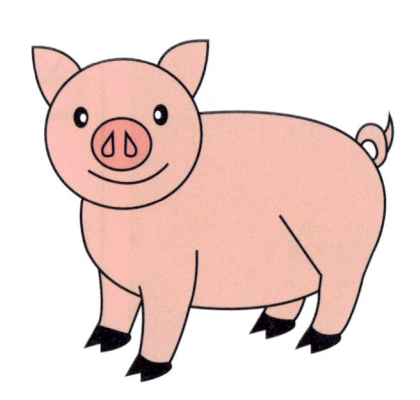

This | is | my | big

pig

This is my pig.

This is my big pig.

12

Lesson 4A - Decoding

Instructor's Guide

DURATION:
3-5 days

OBJECTIVES:
- Produce and memorize sound for letters :
  l, i, d, k, h
- Blend sounds to decode cvc words.

Day 1-2
Instruct child to make the sound of each letter as they run their fingers across letters to learn and memorize the sounds
eg. l i d
Repeat several times.
Then randomly touch letter and instruct child to make the letter sound.
e.g. i h k

Day 3-5
Instruct child to make the sounds and blend at the end
e.g. l i d
lid

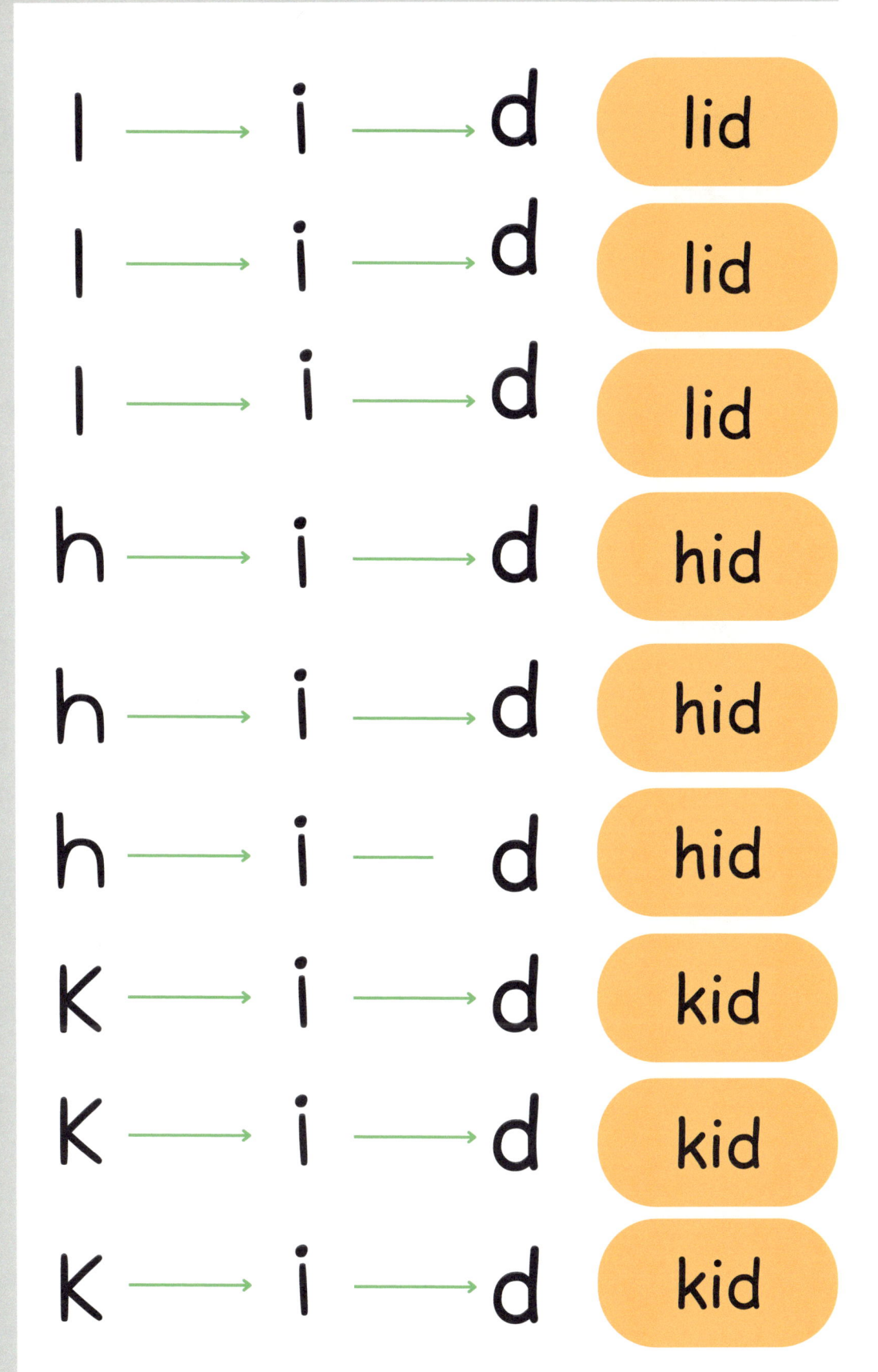

l → i → d   lid
l → i → d   lid
l → i → d   lid
h → i → d   hid
h → i → d   hid
h → i — d   hid
K → i → d   kid
K → i → d   kid
K → i → d   kid

Lesson 4B- Sight Words

Instructor's Guide

DURATION:
2 days

OBJECTIVE:
- Memorize the words 'here' and 'it'.

Instruct child to touch and say the words left to right. Repeat several times. Touch words randomly and instruct child say the words.

Here	it	here
Here	it	here
Here	it	here

Instruct child to colour all 'here' in a colour of their choice and all 'it' in another colour of their choice.

Here it

here it

it Here

Here

here it

14

Lesson 4C - Reading

Instructor's Guide

DURATION:
2-3 days

OBJECTIVES:
- Read phrases and sentences given.
- Read for meaning.

Instruct child to read the phrases and sentences. Repeat several times.

Instruct child to identify and circle the picture that matches the sentence read.

Here is the

the lid

Here is it.

The kid hid the lid here.

15

Match the words to the picture

lid

pig

wig

kid

Circle the picture that the word matches.

big

Track Progress

This is my pig.
My pig is big.
My big pig can dig.
The kid hid the lid.
The big pig is on the lid.

" 1. What is big?

2. Where did the kid hide the lid? "

Evaluation Table	1	2	3
Decoding Skill			
Sight Word Recognition			
Comprehension			
Comment :			

Review

Touch and say the words

bat	can	big	bid
cat	man	dig	hid
mat	ran	pig	kid
sat	tan	wig	lid
rat	van		rid

| the | my | is | it |
| on | here | in | this |

Read the sentences.

The cat sat on the mat.

The man is in the van.

This is my big pig.

The kid hid the lid here.

Lesson 5A - Decoding

Instructor's Guide

DURATION:
3-5 days

OBJECTIVES:
- Produce and memorize sound for letters :
  b, r, f, e, d
- Blend sounds to decode cvc words.

Day 1-2
Instruct child to make the sound of each letter as they run their fingers across letters to learn and memorize the sounds
eg. b e d
Repeat several times. Then randomly touch letter and instruct child to make the letter sound.
e.g. f d b

Day 3-5
Instruct child to make the sounds and blend at the end
e.g. b e d
bed

b → e → d   bed
b → e → d   bed
b → e → d   bed
r → e → d   red
r → e → d   red
r → e — d   red
f → e → d   fed
f → e → d   fed
f → e → d   fed

19

Lesson 5B- Sight Words

Instructor's Guide

DURATION:
2 days

OBJECTIVE:
- Memorize the words 'little' and 'I'.

Instruct child to touch and say the words left to right. Repeat several times. Touch words randomly and instruct child say the words.

Instruct child to colour all 'little' in a colour of their choice and all 'I' in another colour of their choice.

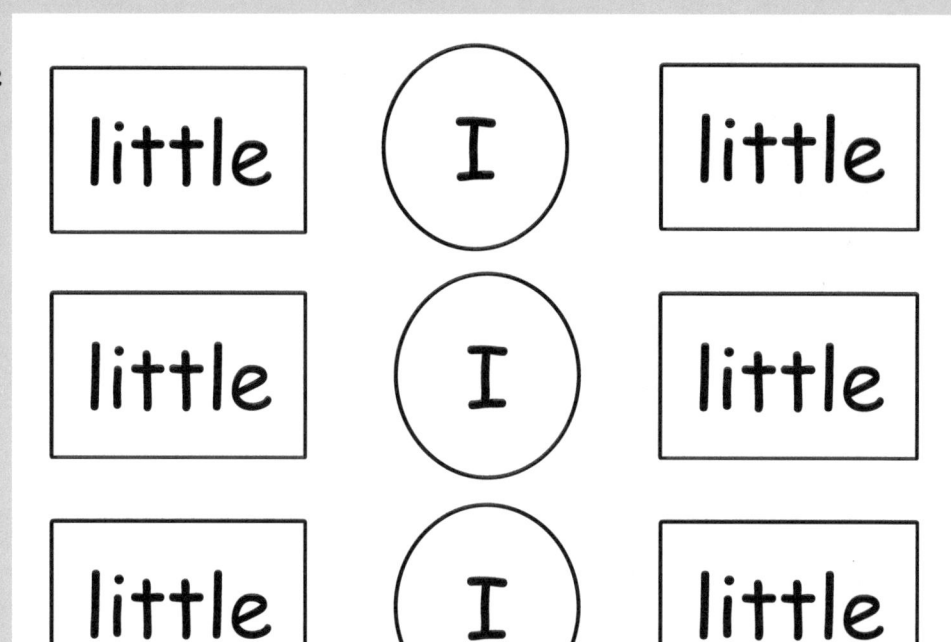

little	I	little
little	I	little
little	I	little

little
I
I
little
little
little
I
I
little

20

Lesson 5C - Reading

Instructor's Guide

DURATION:
2-3 days

OBJECTIVES:
- Read phrases and sentences given.
- Read for meaning.

Instruct child to read the phrases and sentences. Repeat several times.

Instruct child to identify and circle the picture that matches the sentence read.

I fed   Ted on   the bed

I fed Ted.

I fed Ted on the little bed.

21

Lesson 6A - Decoding

Instructor's Guide

DURATION:
3-5 days

OBJECTIVES:
- Produce and memorize sound for letters:
  j, e, t, p, w
- Blend sounds to decode cvc words.

Day 1-2
Instruct child to make the sound of each letter as they run their fingers across letters to learn and memorize the sounds
eg. j e t
Repeat several times.
Then randomly touch letter and instruct child to make the letter sound.
e.g. w t p

Day 3-5
Instruct child to make the sounds and blend at the end
e.g. j e t
jet

j → e → t   jet
j → e → t   jet
j → e → t   jet
p → e → t   pet
p → e → t   pet
p → e — t   pet
w → e → t   wet
w → e → t   wet
w → e → t   wet

22

Lesson 6B - Sight Words

Instructor's Guide

DURATION:
2 days

OBJECTIVE:
- Memorize the words 'look' and 'at'.

Instruct child to touch and say the words left to right. Repeat several times. Touch words randomly and instruct child say the words.

Instruct child to colour all 'look' in a colour of their choice and all 'at' in another colour of their choice.

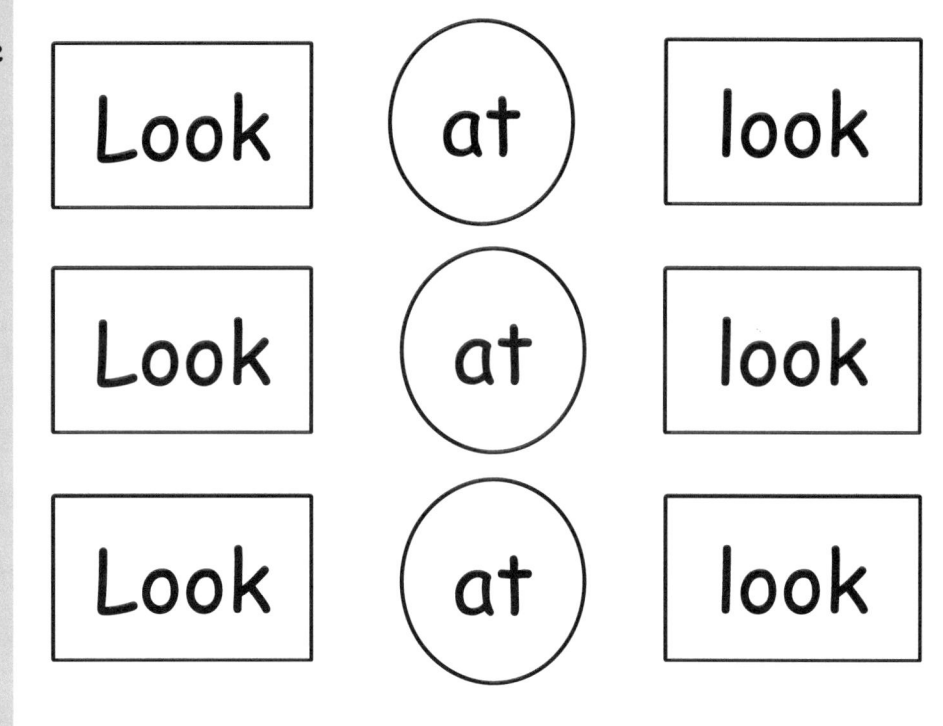

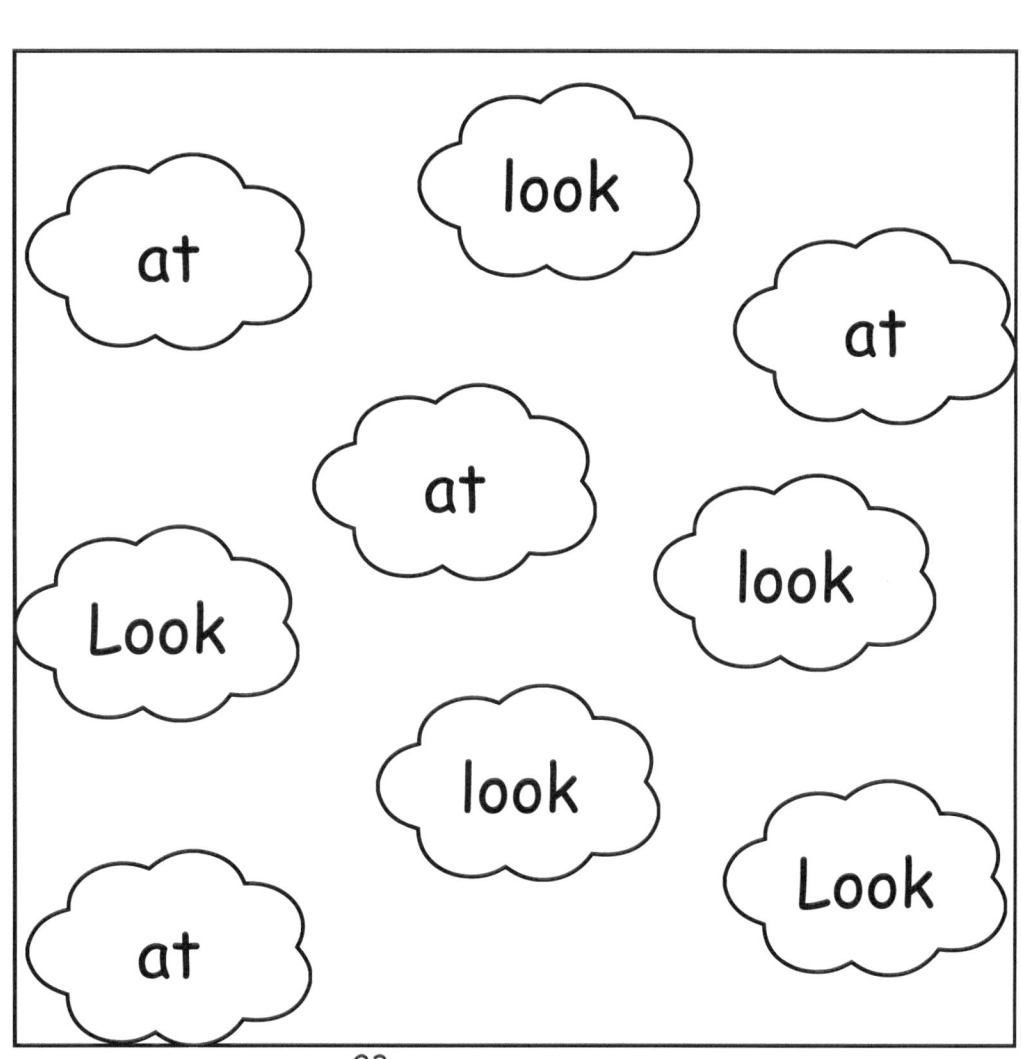

Look	at	look
Look	at	look
Look	at	look

at

look

at

at

Look

look

look

Look

at

Lesson 6C - Reading

Instructor's Guide

DURATION:
2-3 days

OBJECTIVES:
- Read phrases and sentences given.
- Read for meaning.

Instruct child to read the phrases and sentences. Repeat several times.

Instruct child to identify and circle the picture that matches the sentence read.

Look at   wet cat

on the jet

Look   at   my   pet.

Look   at   the   wet   pet on   the   jet.

24

Match the words to the picture

jet

bed

net

pet

Colour the starfish.

red

Track Progress

Look at Ted.
Ted is wet.
The wet pet is on the little jet.
I fed Ted on the little jet.

"
1. What is the name of the pet?
2. Why do you think the pet is on the jet?
"

Evaluation Table	1	2	3
Decoding Skill			
Sight Word Recognition			
Comprehension			
Comment :			

Lesson 7A - Decoding

Instructor's Guide

DURATION:
3-5 days

OBJECTIVES:
- Produce and memorize sound for letters:
  b, o, x, f, p
- Blend sounds to decode cvc words.

Day 1-2
Instruct child to make the sound of each letter as they run their fingers across letters to learn and memorize the sounds
eg. b o x
Repeat several times.
Then randomly touch letter and instruct child to make the letter sound.
e.g. f x o

Day 3-5
Instruct child to make the sounds and blend at the end
e.g. b o x
box

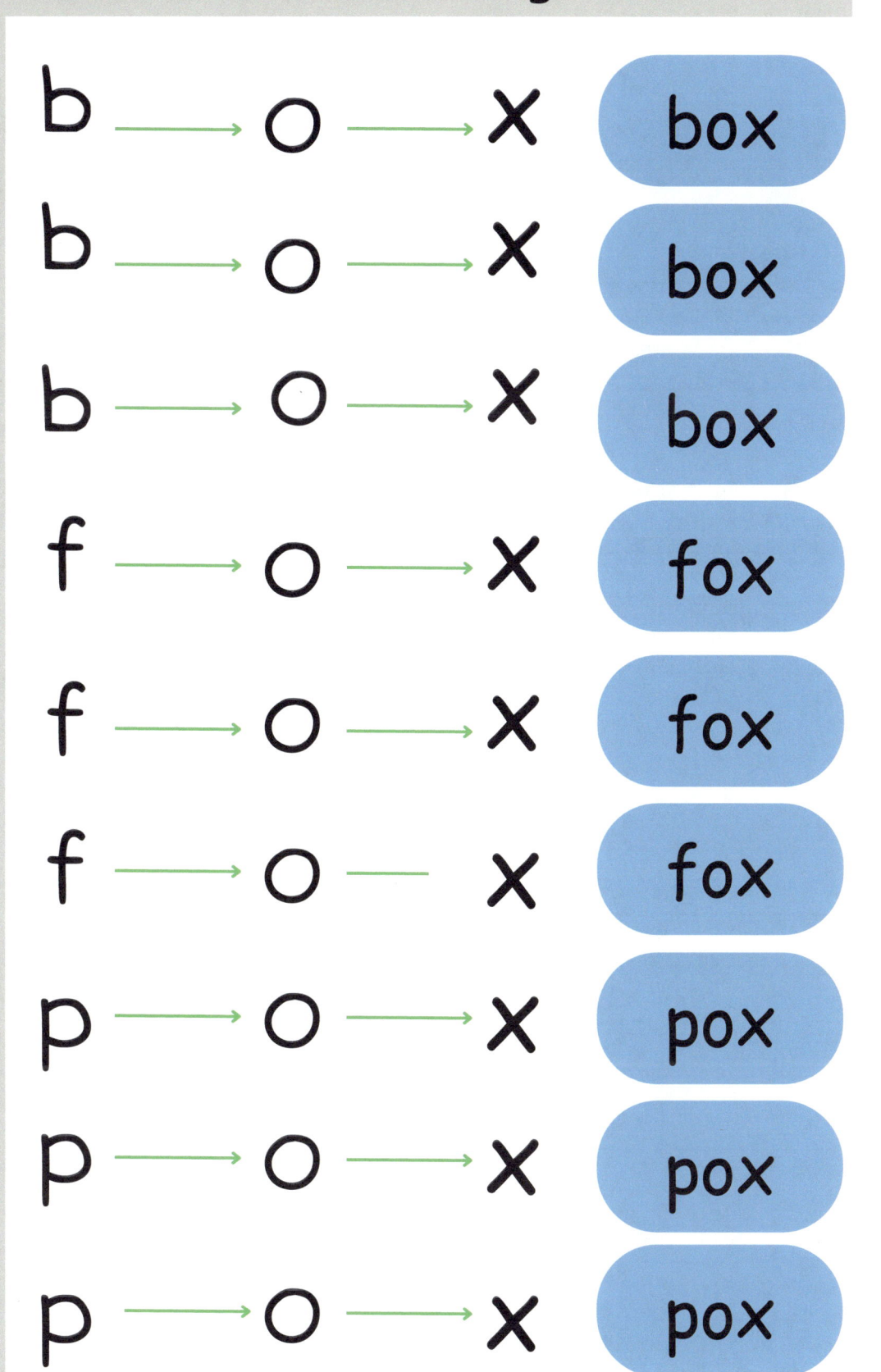

b → o → x   box
b → o → x   box
b → o → x   box
f → o → x   fox
f → o → x   fox
f → o — x   fox
p → o → x   pox
p → o → x   pox
p → o → x   pox

27

Lesson 7B- Sight Words

Instructor's Guide

DURATION:
2 days

OBJECTIVE:
- Memorize the words 'play' and 'with'.

Instruct child to touch and say the words left to right. Repeat several times. Touch words randomly and instruct child say the words.

Instruct child to colour all 'play' in a colour of their choice and all 'with' in another colour of their choice.

play	with
play	with
play	with

- with
- play
- play
- play
- with
- with
- with
- play
- play

28

Lesson 7C - Reading

Instructor's Guide

DURATION:
2-3 days

OBJECTIVES:
- Read phrases and sentences given.
- Read for meaning.

Instruct child to read the phrases and sentences. Repeat several times.

Instruct child to identify and circle the picture that matches the sentence read.

| Look | at | | little | fox |
| play | with | | big | box |

Look at the little fox.

Look. The little fox can play with the big box.

29

Lesson 8A - Decoding

Instructor's Guide

DURATION:
3-5 days

OBJECTIVES:
- Produce and memorize sound for letters :
  h, o, p, m, t
- Blend sounds to decode cvc words.

Day 1
Instruct child to make the sound of each letter as they run their fingers across letters to learn and memorize the sounds
eg. h o p
Repeat several times.
Then randomly touch letter and instruct child to make the letter sound.
e.g. p m t

Day 2-3
Instruct child to make the sounds and blend at the end
e.g.   h o p
hop

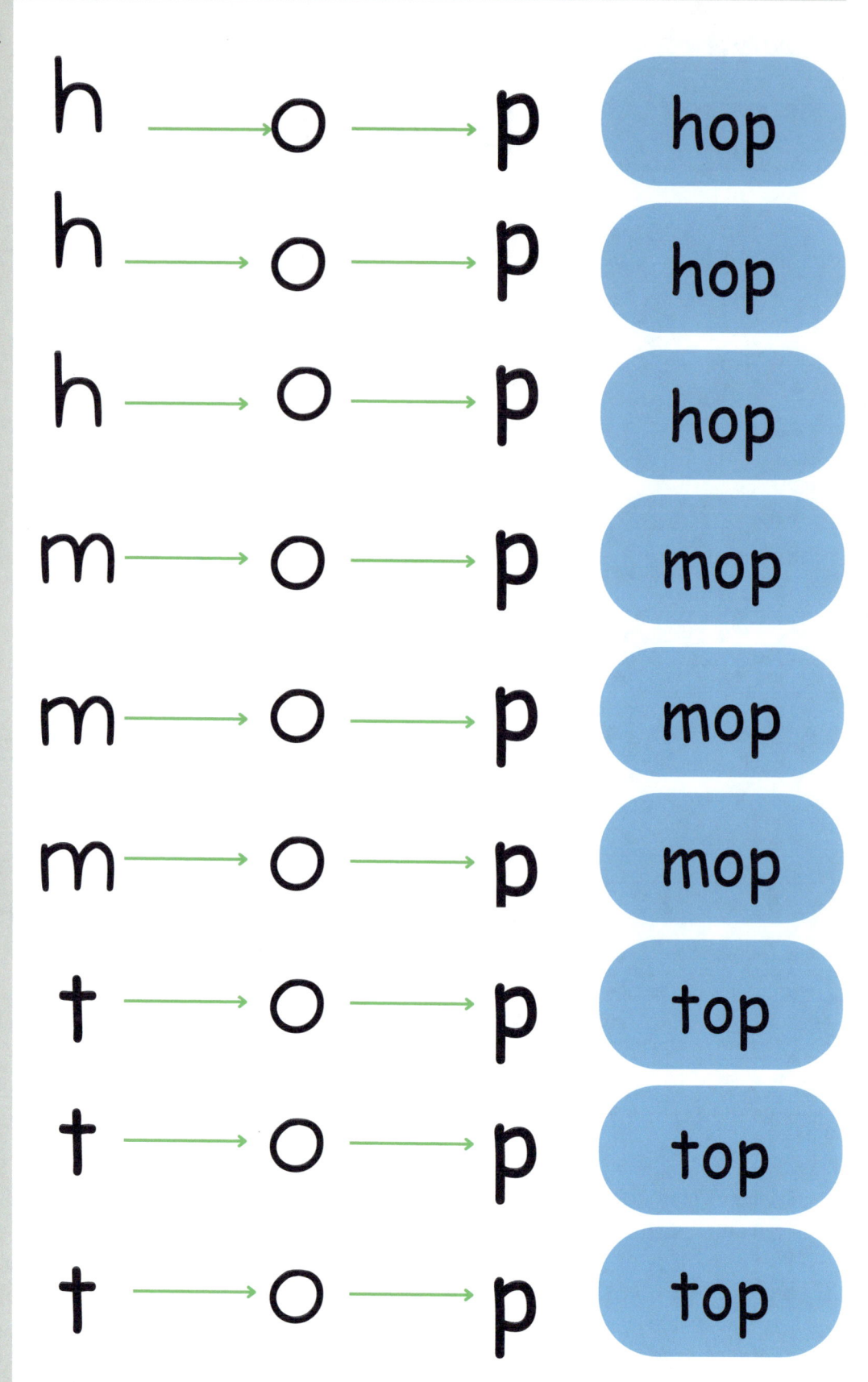

h → o → p   hop
h → o → p   hop
h → o → p   hop
m → o → p   mop
m → o → p   mop
m → o → p   mop
t → o → p   top
t → o → p   top
t → o → p   top

30

Lesson 8B- Sight Words

Instructor's Guide

DURATION:
2 days

OBJECTIVE:
- Memorize the words 'and' and 'we'.

Instruct child to touch and say the words left to right. Repeat several times. Touch words randomly and instruct child say the words.

Instruct child to colour all 'and' in a colour of their choice and all 'we' in another colour of their choice.

and	we
and	we
and	we

and / we / and / we / we / and / we / and / and

Lesson 8C - Reading

Instructor's Guide

DURATION:
2-3 days

OBJECTIVES:
- Read phrases and sentences given.
- Read for meaning.

| we | can | | mop | and |

| hop |

We can mop the top.

We can mop and hop.

Instruct child to read the phrases and sentences. Repeat several times.

Instruct child to identify and circle the picture that matches the sentence read.

32

Match the words to the picture

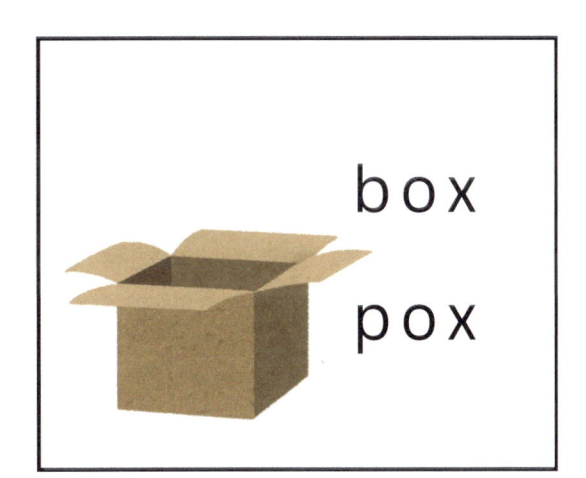

pop
mop

box
pox

pox
pop

box
fox

Track Progress

We can mop.
We can mop and hop.

We play with the box.
We play with the box and the fox.

❝
1. What did they play with?

2. What can you use a mop to do?
❞

Evaluation Table	1	2	3
Decoding Skill			
Sight Word Recognition			
Comprehension			
Comment :			

Review

Touch and say the words

bed	jet	box	cop
fed	met	fox	hop
red	pet	pox	mop
Ted	wet		pop
	vet		top

little	I	look	at
play	with	and	we

Read the sentences.

I fed Ted on the little bed.

Look at the wet pet on the jet.

The little fox can play with the big box.

Lesson 9A - Decoding

Instructor's Guide

DURATION:
3-5 days

OBJECTIVES:
- Produce and memorize sound for letters : b, u, g, r, j
- Blend sounds to decode cvc words.

Day 1-2
Instruct child to make the sound of each letter as they run their fingers across letters to learn and memorize the sounds
eg. b u g
Repeat several times.
Then randomly touch letter and instruct child to make the letter sound.
e.g. g j u

Day 3-5
Instruct child to make the sounds and blend at the end
e.g.   b u g
bug

b → u → g   bug
b → u → g   bug
b → u → g   bug
j → u → g   jug
j → u → g   jug
j → u → g   jug
r → u → g   rug
r → u → g   rug
r → u → g   rug

36

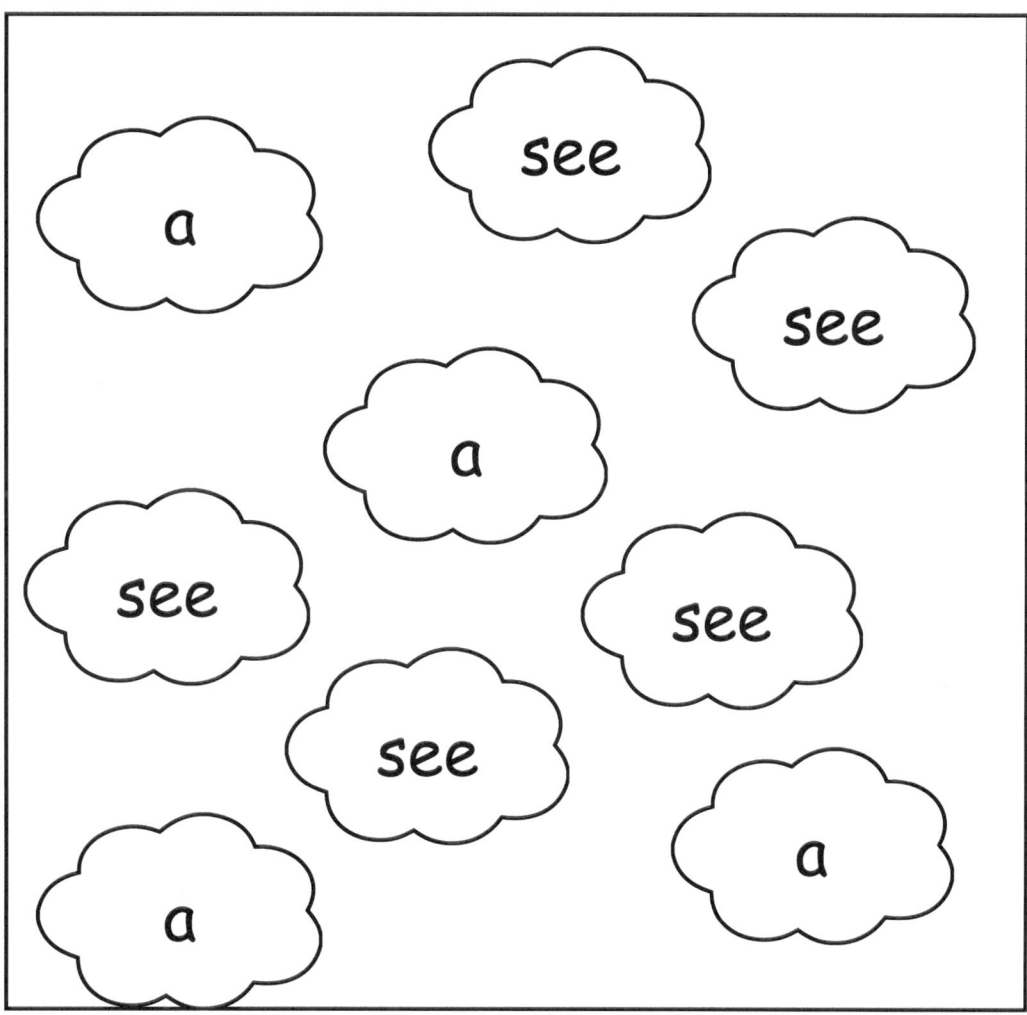

Lesson 9B - Sight Words

Instructor's Guide

DURATION:
2 days

OBJECTIVE:
- Memorize the words 'see' and 'a'.

Instruct child to touch and say the words left to right. Repeat several times. Touch words randomly and instruct child say the words.

see	a
see	a
see	a

Instruct child to colour all 'see' in a colour of their choice and all 'a' in another colour of their choice.

(Clouds containing: a, see, see, a, see, see, see, a, a)

Lesson 9C - Reading

Instructor's Guide

DURATION:
2-3 days

OBJECTIVES:
- Read phrases and sentences given.
- Read for meaning.

Instruct child to read the phrases and sentences. Repeat several times.

Instruct child to identify and circle the picture that matches the sentence read.

| we | can | | mop | and |

| hop |

I see a red bug.

I see a red bug with a jug

38

Lesson 10A - Decoding

Instructor's Guide

DURATION:
3-5 days

OBJECTIVES:
- Produce and memorize sound for letters: f, u, n, r, s
- Blend sounds to decode cvc words.

Day 1-2
Instruct child to make the sound of each letter as they run their fingers across letters to learn and memorize the sounds
eg. f u n
Repeat several times.
Then randomly touch letter and instruct child to make the letter sound.
e.g. n u s

Day 3-5
Instruct child to make the sounds and blend at the end
e.g. f u n
fun

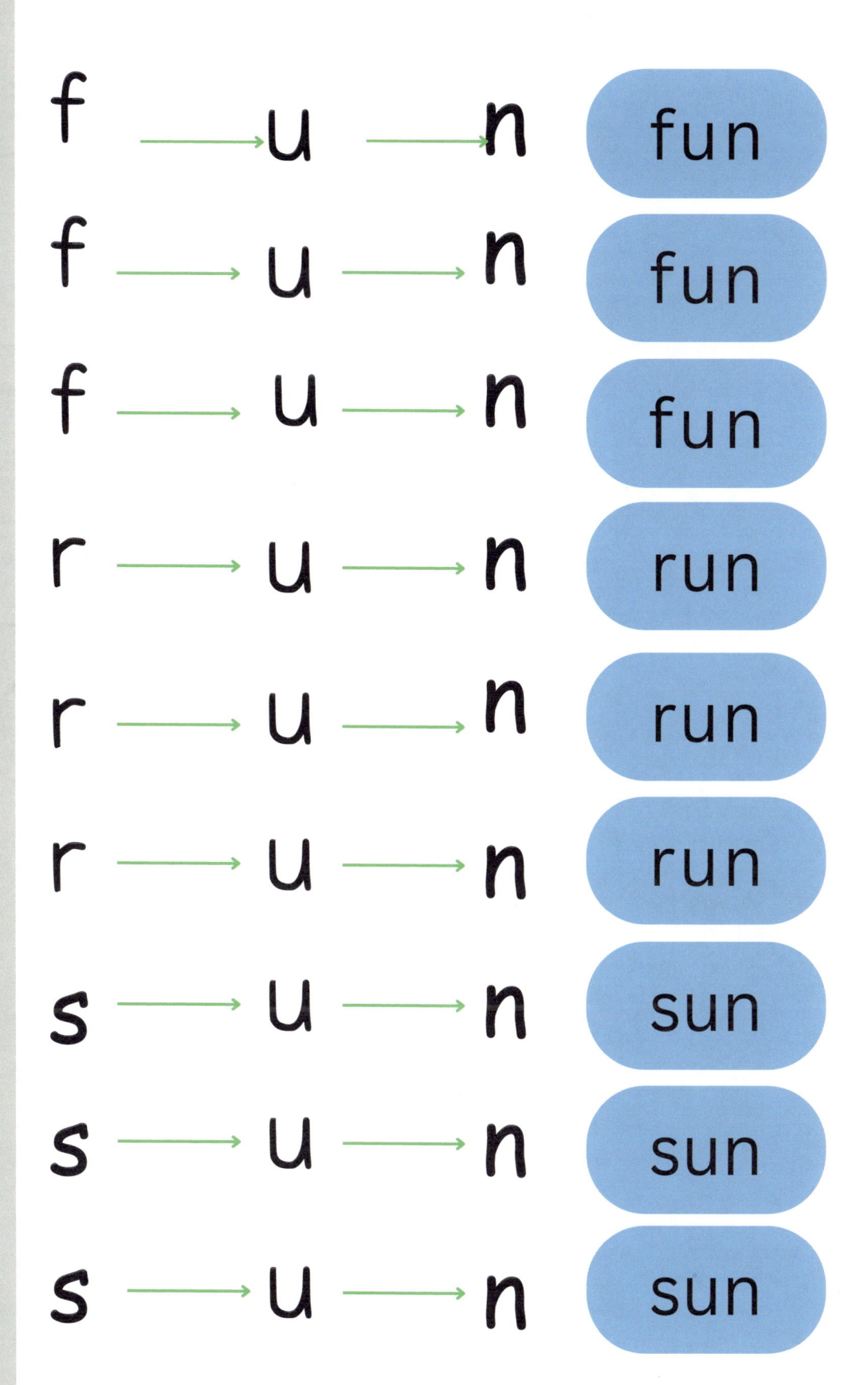

f	u	n	fun
f	u	n	fun
f	u	n	fun
r	u	n	run
r	u	n	run
r	u	n	run
s	u	n	sun
s	u	n	sun
s	u	n	sun

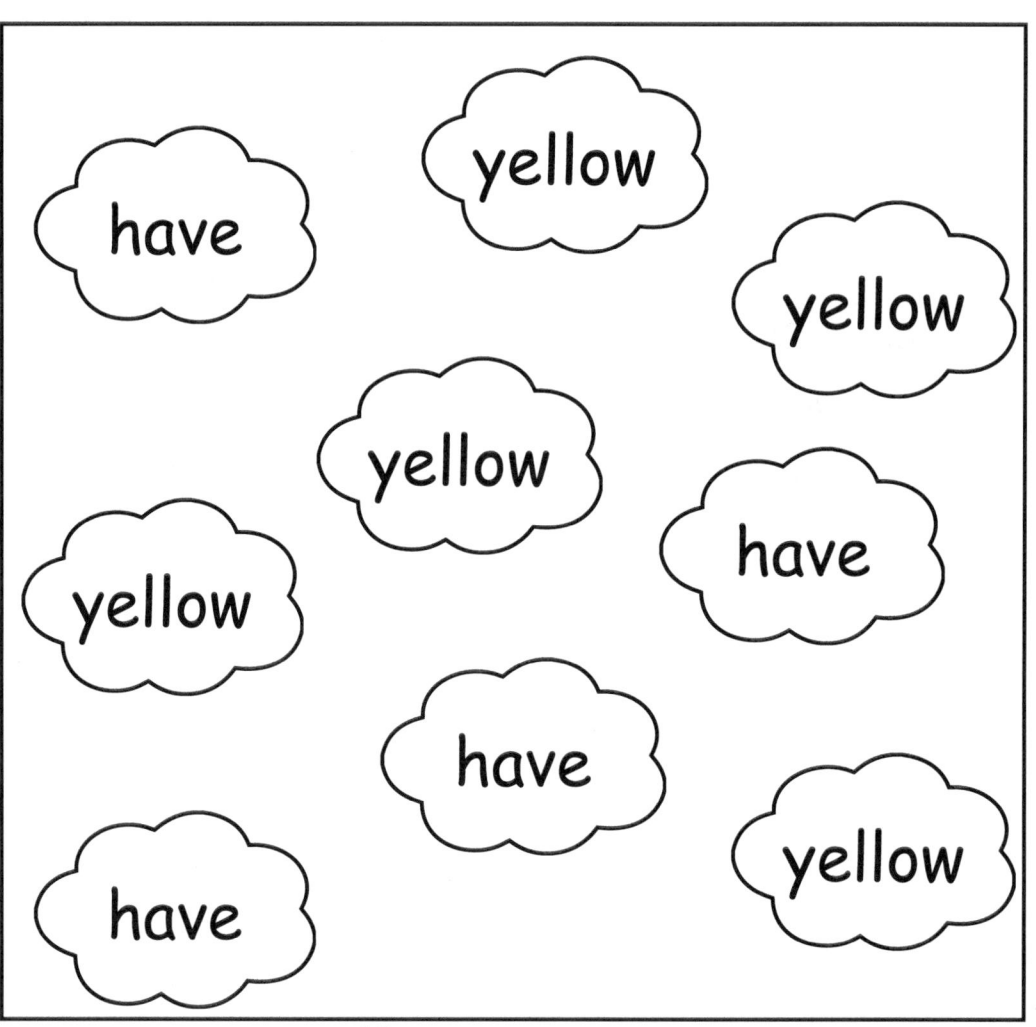

Lesson 10B- Sight Words

Instructor's Guide

DURATION:
2 days

OBJECTIVE:
- Memorize the words 'have' and 'yellow'.

Instruct child to touch and say the words left to right. Repeat several times. Touch words randomly and instruct child say the words.

Instruct child to colour all 'have' in a colour of their choice and all 'yellow' in another colour of their choice.

have	yellow
have	yellow
have	yellow

have
yellow
yellow
have
yellow
yellow
have
have
yellow

Lesson 10C - Reading

Instructor's Guide

DURATION:
2-3 days

OBJECTIVES:
- Read phrases and sentences given.
- Read for meaning.

Instruct child to read the phrases and sentences. Repeat several times.

| we | run | | and | have |

| fun |

We have fun in the yellow sun.

We run and have fun in the sun.

Instruct child to identify and circle the picture that matches the sentence read.

41

Match the words to the picture

jug
bug

sun
fun

mug
rug

run
bun

Track Progress

We run in the sun.
We run and have fun in the sun.
I see a red bug.
I see a red bug in a red jug.

" 1. What is the colour of the bug?
2. What else can they do to have fun? "

Evaluation Table	1	2	3
Decoding Skill			
Sight Word Recognition			
Comprehension			
Comment :			

Unit Review
Make the letter sound

s m a t c

r v n b p

d w l k e

f j o u x

h g

Decoding Review

Say these words.

sat	big	bed	box	bug
cat	pig	red	fox	rug
mat	wig	fed	pox	jug
ran	lid	jet	hop	fun
man	kid	pet	mop	run
van	hid	wet	top	sun

Bonus words

Decode these words.

can	bid	get	dot	bun
fat	fit	hen	got	gum
mad	sit	men	jog	hut
sad	pin	ten	not	pug
rag	tin	beg	rod	mud

Sight Word Review
Say these words.

the	this	little	play	see
on	my	I	with	a
is	here	look	and	have
in	it	at	we	yellow

Read the sentences

I see a little. yellow rag. Look at it. We can play with it. My pet can get in the big box and play the mud.
We have fun.

UNIT 2
CVCC
Short Vowel

Lesson 11A - Decoding

Instructor's Guide

DURATION:
3-5 days

OBJECTIVES:
- Blend sounds to create cvcc words ending with /ck/.

Day 1-2

Instruct child to make the sounds and blend at the end.
e.g. b a ck   back

N.B. Remember the 'ck' only makes one sound /c/.

Day 3-5
Decode words in orange bubble.
e.g   back

b → a → ck	back
h → a → ck	hack
J → a → ck	Jack
l → a → ck	lack
p → a → ck	pack
r → a → ck	rack
s → a → ck	sack
t → a → ck	tack
w → a → ck	wack

48

Lesson 11B- Sight Words

Instructor's Guide

DURATION:
2 days

OBJECTIVE:
- Memorize the words 'has' and 'his'.

Instruct child to touch and say the words left to right. Repeat several times. Touch words randomly and instruct child say the words.

Instruct child to colour all 'has' in a colour of their choice and all 'have' in another colour of their choice.

has	his
has	his
has	his

- his
- has
- his
- has
- his
- has
- his
- has
- has

Lesson 11C - Reading

Instructor's Guide

DURATION:
2-3 days

OBJECTIVES:
- Read phrases and sentences given.
- Read for meaning.

Instruct child to read the phrases and sentences. Repeat several times.

Instruct child to identify and circle the picture that matches the sentence read.

Jack has a yellow rack.

Jack has his yellow rack in a red sack.

Jack has the red sack on his back.

Lesson 12A - Decoding

Instructor's Guide

DURATION:
3-5 days

OBJECTIVES:
- Blend sounds to create cvcc words ending with /ck/.

Day 1-2

Instruct child to make the sounds and blend at the end.
e.g. p i ck   pick

N.B. Remember the 'ck' only makes one sound /c/.

Day 3-5
Decode words in orange bubble.
e.g   pick

k → i → ck   kick
l → i → ck   lick
N → i → ck   Nick
p → i → ck   pick
s → i → ck   sick
b → e → ck   beck
d → e → ck   deck
n → e → ck   neck
p → e → ck   peck

Lesson 12B - Sight Words

Instructor's Guide

DURATION:
2 days

OBJECTIVE:
- Memorize the words 'fell' and 'down'.

Instruct child to touch and say the words left to right. Repeat several times. Touch words randomly and instruct child say the words.

Instruct child to colour all 'fell' in a colour of their choice and all 'down' in another colour of their choice.

fell	down
fell	down
fell	down

fell
down
fell
down
down
down
fell
fell
down

Lesson 12C - Reading

Instructor's Guide

DURATION:
2-3 days

OBJECTIVES:
- Read phrases and sentences given.
- Read for meaning.

Instruct child to read the phrases and sentences. Repeat several times.

Instruct child to identify and circle the picture that matches the sentence read.

Nick fell down.

Nick can kick and pick.

Nick fell down on his neck.

Nick is sick.

Lesson 13A - Decoding

Instructor's Guide

DURATION:
3-5 days

OBJECTIVES:
- Blend sounds to create cvcc words ending with /ck/.

Day 1-2

Instruct child to make the sounds and blend at the end.
e.g. m o ck   mock

N.B. Remember the 'ck' only makes one sound /c/.

Day 3-5
Decode words in orange bubble.
e.g   mock

d → o → ck   dock

l → o → ck   lock

m → o → ck   mock

r → o → ck   rock

s → o → ck   sock

b → u → ck   buck

d → u → ck   duck

l → u → ck   luck

y → u → ck   yuck

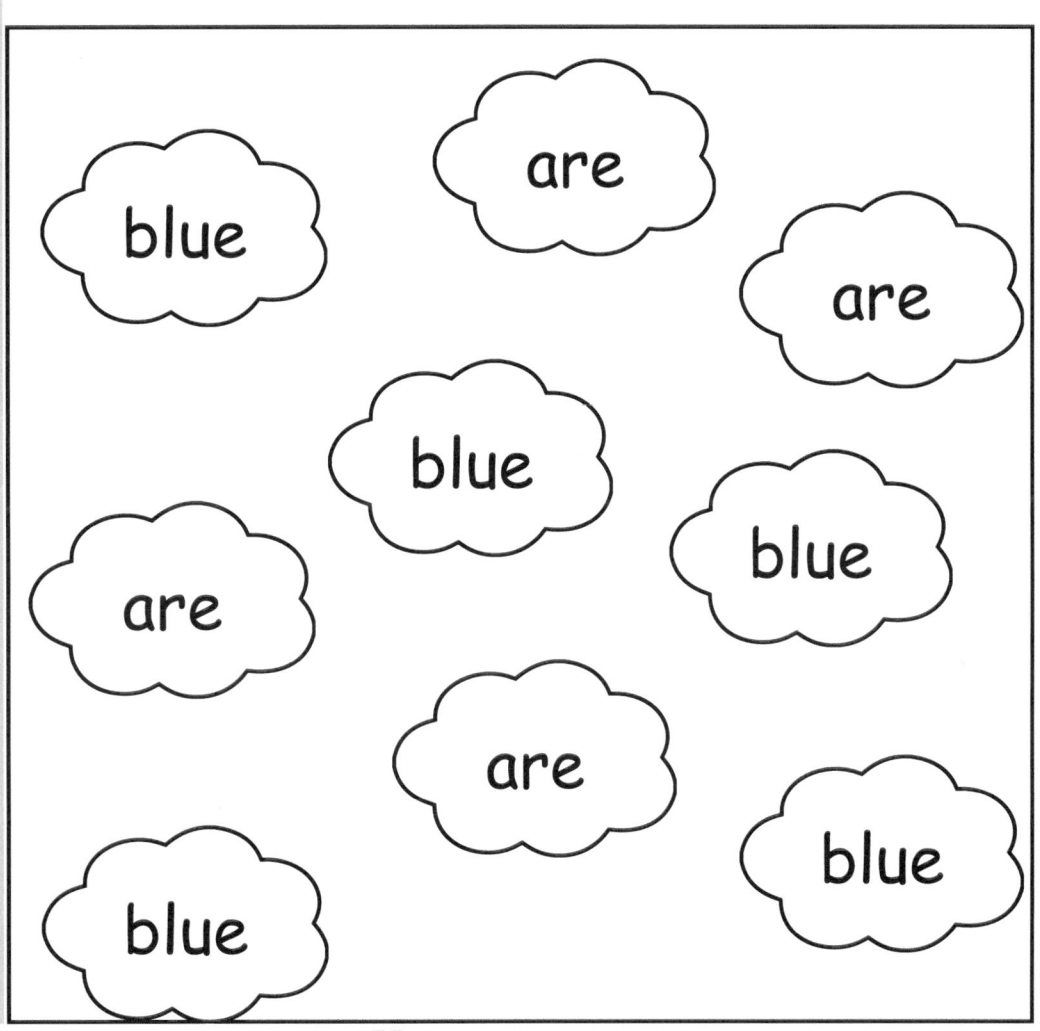

Lesson 13B- Sight Words

Instructor's Guide

DURATION:
2 days

OBJECTIVE:
- Memorize the words 'blue' and 'are'.

Instruct child to touch and say the words left to right. Repeat several times. Touch words randomly and instruct child say the words.

Instruct child to colour all 'blue' in a colour of their choice and all 'are' in another colour of their choice.

blue	are
blue	are
blue	are

blue are are blue are blue blue are blue

55

Lesson 13C - Reading

Instructor's Guide

DURATION:
2-3 days

OBJECTIVES:
- Read phrases and sentences given.
- Read for meaning.

Instruct child to read the phrases and sentences. Repeat several times.

Instruct child to identify and circle the picture that matches the sentence read.

I have a rock .
I have a sock .

My sock and my rock are blue .

Look at the duck.
The duck has my little blue sock.

Track Progress

Jack fell down.

Jack fell down and hit his neck.

Jack hit his neck on the rock.

Jack is sick.

❝
1. Where did Jack hit his neck?

2. Why do you think Jack fell down?
❞

Evaluation Table	1	2	3
Decoding Skill			
Sight Word Recognition			
Comprehension			
Comment :			

Lesson 14A - Decoding

Instructor's Guide

DURATION:
3-5 days

OBJECTIVES:
- Blend sounds to create cvcc words ending with /ss/.

Day 1-2

Instruct child to make the sounds and blend at the end.
e.g. p a ss   pass

N.B. Remember the 'same' only makes one sound /c/.

Day 3-5
Decode words in orange bubble.
e.g   pass

b → a → ss   bass

m → a → ss   mass

p → a → ss   pass

h → i → ss   hiss

k → i → ss   kiss

m → i → ss   miss

l → e → ss   less

m → e → ss   mess

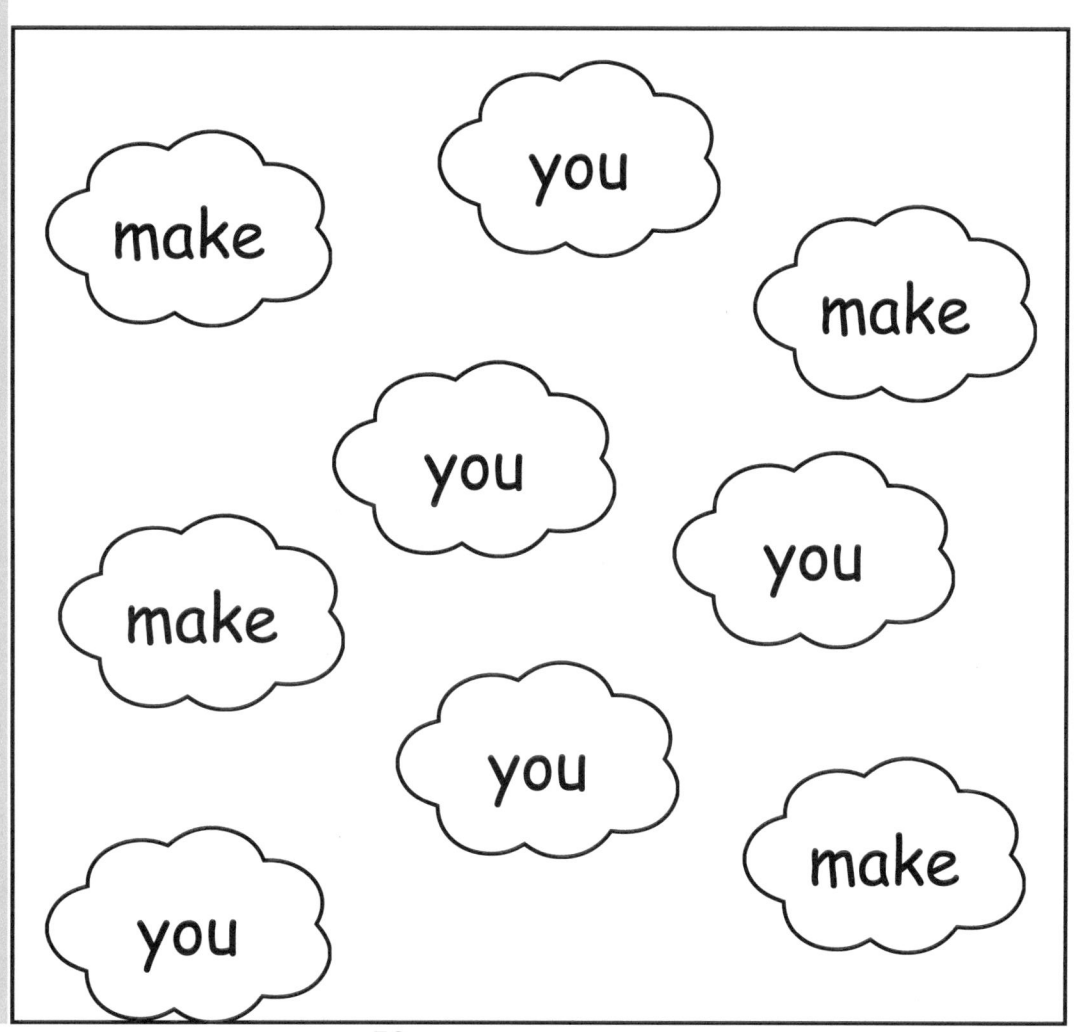

Lesson 14B- Sight Words

Instructor's Guide

DURATION:
2 days

OBJECTIVE:
- Memorize the words 'have' and 'yellow'.

Instruct child to touch and say the words left to right. Repeat several times. Touch words randomly and instruct child say the words.

Instruct child to colour all 'have' in a colour of their choice and all 'yellow' in another colour of their choice.

you	make
you	make
you	make

make · you · make · you · you · make · you · you · make · you

59

Lesson 14C - Reading

Instructor's Guide

DURATION:
2-3 days

OBJECTIVES:
- Read phrases and sentences given.
- Read for meaning.

Instruct child to read the phrases and sentences. Repeat several times.

Instruct child to identify and circle the picture that matches the sentence read.

I can make a mess.
You can make a mess.

You can pass the mop.
I can mop the mess.

60

Review

Touch and say the words

back	lock
pack	rock
pick	sock
sick	duck
neck	luck

bass	kiss
mass	miss
pass	less
loss	mess
hiss	mess

his	fell
has	down

blue	you
are	make

Read the sentences.

Jack has a ig lock on his blue bag pack. It has a rock and a rack in it. It fell in the mess.

Lesson 15A - Decoding

b → a → n → d   **band**

h → a → n → d   **hand**

l → a → n → d   **land**

w → a → n → d   **wand**

b → e → n → d   **bend**

l → e → n → d   **lend**

m → e → n → d   **mend**

s → e → n → d   **send**

Lesson 15A - Decoding

b → o → n → d   bond

f → o → n → d   fond

p → o → n → d   pond

f → u → n → d   fund

Lesson 15B- Sight Words

Instructor's Guide

DURATION:
2 days

OBJECTIVE:
- Memorize the words 'he' and 'not'.

Instruct child to touch and say the words left to right. Repeat several times. Touch words randomly and instruct child say the words.

Instruct child to colour all 'he' in a colour of their choice and all 'not' in another colour of their choice.

He	not
he	not
he	not

he
not
he
he
not
not
not
he
he

Lesson 15C - Reading

Instructor's Guide

DURATION:
2-3 days

OBJECTIVES:
- Read phrases and sentences given.
- Read for meaning.

Instruct child to read the phrases and sentences. Repeat several times.

Instruct child to identify and circle the picture that matches the sentence read.

The band is fun.
I am in the band.

He is not in the band with me.

He can lend us a hand in the band.

Lesson 16A- Decoding

r → a → f → t   raft

l → e → f → t   left

l → i → f → t   lift

g → i → f → t   gift

r → i → f → t   rift

s → i → f → t   sift

l → o → f → t   loft

s → o → f → t   soft

Lesson 16B- Sight Words

Instructor's Guide

DURATION:
2 days

OBJECTIVE:
- Memorize the words 'go' and 'find'.

Instruct child to touch and say the words left to right. Repeat several times. Touch words randomly and instruct child say the words.

Instruct child to colour all 'go' in a colour of their choice and all 'find' in another colour of their choice.

Go	find
go	find
go	find

Go   find   go
   find
go   find
     go
find   Go

Lesson 16C - Reading

Instructor's Guide

DURATION:
2-3 days

OBJECTIVES:
- Read phrases and sentences given.
- Read for meaning.

Instruct child to read the phrases and sentences. Repeat several times.

Instruct child to identify and circle the picture that matches the sentence read.

Go find the gift.
You can go left.

You can go left to find the raft.
Did you see the gift?

68

Track Progress

I see the land.
Nick will find the pond.
We are at the pond.
The sand is soft and hot.
We play on the raft in the pond.

"
1. Who will find the pond?

2. Why do you think the sand is hot?
"

Evaluation Table	1	2	3
Decoding Skill			
Sight Word Recognition			
Comprehension			
Comment :			

Lesson 17A - Decoding

f → a → s → t   fast

l → a → s → t   last

p → a → s → t   past

v → a → s → t   vast

b → e → s → t   best

r → e → s → t   rest

t → e → s → t   test

w → e → s → t   west

Lesson 17A - Decoding

f → i → s → t　　　fist

l → i → s → t　　　list

m → i → s → t　　　mist

c → o → s → t　　　cost

l → o → s → t　　　lost

j → u → s → t　　　dust

m → u → s → t　　　must

r → u → s → t　　　rust

Lesson 17B - Sight Words

Instructor's Guide

DURATION:
2 days

OBJECTIVE:
- Memorize the words 'she' and 'her'.

Instruct child to touch and say the words left to right. Repeat several times. Touch words randomly and instruct child say the words.

Instruct child to colour all 'she' in a colour of their choice and all 'her' in another colour of their choice.

She	her
she	her
she	her

- Her
- she
- her
- her
- she
- She
- she
- her
- her

Lesson 17C - Reading

Instructor's Guide

DURATION:
2-3 days

OBJECTIVES:
- Read phrases and sentences given.
- Read for meaning.

Instruct child to read the phrases and sentences. Repeat several times.

Instruct child to identify and circle the picture that matches the sentence read.

Did she find the list? It has the best cost.

She did the best on the test. So, she must get the fast car.

Lesson 18A- Decoding

a → s → k   ask

b → a → s → k   bask

m → a → s → k   mask

t → a → s → k   task

d → e → s → k   desk

d → i → s → k   disk

r → i → s → k   risk

t → u → s → k   tusk

Lesson 18B - Sight Words

Instructor's Guide

DURATION:
2 days

OBJECTIVE:
- Memorize the words 'now' and 'new'.

Instruct child to touch and say the words left to right. Repeat several times. Touch words randomly and instruct child say the words.

Instruct child to colour all 'now' in a colour of their choice and all 'new' in another colour of their choice.

Now	New
now	new
now	new

new, now, now, new, new, Now, now, New, new

Lesson 18C - Reading

Instructor's Guide

DURATION:
2-3 days

OBJECTIVES:
- Read phrases and sentences given.
- Read for meaning.

Instruct child to read the phrases and sentences. Repeat several times.

Instruct child to identify and circle the picture that matches the sentence read.

I can ask for a mask.
Now, we have a new mask.

The new mask fell on the desk.
We can dust the desk, now.

Track Progress

Pam and I are at the park.
We find her new car.
We test it on the desk.
It is a fast red and blue car.
She can play with it now.
It is the best.

"
1. Where are the children?

2. Why did they test the car?
"

Evaluation Table	1	2	3
Decoding Skill			
Sight Word Recognition			
Comprehension			
Comment :			

Review

Touch and say the words

hand	raft	last	ask
lend	left	rest	task
send	lift	list	desk
pond	gift	cost	risk
fund	soft	must	tusk

he	go	she	now
not	find	her	new

Read the sentences.

Jack is sick. He must go and get the new raft. Pam will get in the pond. Pam is sick, now. She can rest on the desk.

Sight Word Review

the	I	have	he
on	look	yellow	she
is	at	has	not
in	play	his	go
this	with	fell	find
my	and	down	her
here	we	blue	now
it	see	are	new
little	a	you	big
am	an	make	red

Made in the USA
Columbia, SC
08 October 2024